A Is For Angle

B Is For Black Cat

C Is For Candy

D Is For Devil

E Is For Elf

F Is For Fall

G Is For Ghost

H Is For Halloween

I Is For Idea

J Is For Jack-O'Lantern

K Is For King

L Is For Lantern

M Is For Moon

N Is For Night

O Is For Owl

P Is For Pumpkin

Q Is For Queen

R Is For Robot

S Is For Sweets

T Is For Treat

U Is For Umbrella

V Is For Vampire

W Is For Witch

X Is For XOXO

Y Is For Yummy

Z Is For Zombie

www.ingramcontent.com/pod-product-compliance
Lightning Source LLC
LaVergne TN
LVHW060158080526
838202LV00052B/4165